Original title:
The Bark That Chuckled

Copyright © 2025 Creative Arts Management OÜ
All rights reserved.

Author: Gabriel Kingsley
ISBN HARDBACK: 978-1-80567-418-4
ISBN PAPERBACK: 978-1-80567-717-8

Woodland Whispers of Delight

In the forest where shadows play,
The trees giggle in their own way.
Breezes carry their jokes so light,
While blooms join in with colors bright.

Squirrels chatter with cheeky glee,
Tickling each branch on the old oak tree.
Leaves rustle as laughter spreads wide,
Nature's comedy, we cannot hide.

Leafy Laughter Through the Ages

From ancient roots to tender shoots,
Nature cracks up in tiny boots.
Each acorn drops with a tiny thud,
Creating ripples of giggles and mud.

The wind tells tales that twist and twine,
With whispers of humor in every line.
Across the glade, the giggles bloom,
Beneath the trees, there's always room.

Hilarity Hidden in Mossy Nooks

In the shade where shadows rest,
Fungi chuckle, they're simply the best.
Mossy patches hide secrets of cheer,
Echoes of laughter that all can hear.

Crickets drum with a cheeky beat,
As fireflies dance on tiny feet.
Nature's jesters in emerald coats,
Play tricks and pranks, on little boats.

Chuckles in the Heart of the Grove

Under the canopy, joy spills bright,
Dancing creatures join the light.
Robins tweet with a playful sound,
As the forest bed shakes the ground.

Old logs groan with a funny creak,
Cracking smiles, they're quite the clique.
Butterflies flutter in silly arcs,
Revealing the fun in nature's parks.

Whimsy Woven in the Wilderness

In a realm where giggles grow,
Leaves play tag with winds that blow.
Silly squirrels dance up the trees,
While jabbering jays tease the breeze.

Rabbits wear hats that wobble wide,
While cheeky foxes scamper with pride.
Each branch a stage, each root a jest,
Nature's laughter is truly the best.

The Frolicsome Forest Floor

Mushrooms wearing polka dots,
Laughing at all the sunny spots.
The carpet of leaves makes a sound,
As silly creatures leap all around.

Acorns tumble with a plink,
Squirrels pause just to wink.
Every step is a giggling spree,
Where nature dances joyfully free.

Smirks in the Sun-dappled Shade

Stumps turn to seats for chatting birds,
Chirpy banter without any words.
The sunlight tickles the lurking moss,
While shadows play at being the boss.

Glimmers of laughter slide through the air,
Wiggling worms dangle without a care.
Laughter echoes through branches so tall,
In this merry realm, who wouldn't fall?

Jovial Wind Among the Trees

Whispers of joy ride on the breeze,
Rustling secrets through the leaves with ease.
Swinging vines with a playful tug,
As the old oak gives a hearty shrug.

A squirrel's dance makes the world spin,
With every twirl, it wears a grin.
The trees chuckle, their limbs sway free,
In this joyous play, we all just glee.

Tales of the Chuckling Woods

In a forest where shadows dance,
Trees tell jokes at every chance.
Squirrels laugh with acorn glee,
They giggle loud, beneath the tree.

A rabbit hops with silly grace,
His floppy ears, a comical face.
He trips on roots, then jumps so high,
With laughter echoing in the sky.

A wise old owl has quite the wit,
He hoots and cackles, won't admit.
His feathered friends, they roll in mirth,
Creating joy upon the earth.

At twilight's hush, the critters play,
They chase their shadows, night turns to day.
In this grove of fun and cheer,
The heart of laughter draws us near.

Gleeful Hearts Embedded in the Earth

Beneath the ground, where roots entwine,
Are giggling greens, all in a line.
With every shake, the soil shakes back,
A joyful dance in the whimsical crack.

The worms are wriggling in funny threads,
Spinning tales of two worms' beds.
They chuckle soft as they dig down,
In their secret world beneath the crown.

A toad on a stone starts to croak,
While nearby, a bush starts to poke.
It tickles him just like a feather,
And soon they're laughing all together.

In the patch of light, where daisies bloom,
The ants all march with a comical zoom.
With glee in their tiny, busy hearts,
They build their worlds, full of funny parts.

Where Wood and Wit Intertwine

In the forest where shadows play,
Trees tell jokes at the close of day.
Each knot in the trunk a chuckle bright,
Leaves burst out laughing under the light.

Woodpeckers tap to the rhythm of mirth,
Squirrels spin tales of their own rebirth.
Branches sway with a giggling tune,
Nature's comedians, beneath the moon.

The Cheery Grin of Nature's Canvas.

Beneath the boughs, a giggle grows,
With every breeze, a punchline flows.
Mossy rocks wear a grin so sly,
As daisies wink beneath the sky.

A brook chuckles over smooth, cool stones,
While playful shadows dance on bones.
Whimsical whispers fill up the air,
As flowers laugh without a care.

Whispers of Laughter in the Woods

Among the trees, the spirits play,
Swaying softly, they laugh all day.
A chipmunk's cackle, a deer's light kick,
In this lively realm, time moves quick.

Fungi wear hats, their humor spry,
While beetles spin tales that make you sigh.
Nature's jesters, they roam with glee,
Laughter echoes, wild and free.

Guffaws Beneath the Canopy

In the lush realm where the sun peeks through,
The trees crack jokes—some silly, some blue.
Wildflowers laugh at the bees on a spree,
Nature's jesters, stirring up glee.

A parrot squawks in a melodious song,
While the wind tickles leaves all day long.
Beneath the canopy, fun has no end,
In every corner, there's joy to send.

Merriment Beneath the Old Oak

Under branches wide and grand,
Laughter spills across the land.
Squirrels bounce with sheer delight,
Tickling leaves in morning light.

A wobbly branch starts to sway,
Making shadows dance and play.
Whispers carry, soft and bright,
As the sun begins its flight.

Secrets of the Chuckling Grove

In a grove where secrets hide,
Every tree has wit and pride.
Breezes tease with playful tone,
Nature giggles, never alone.

A knot of roots begins to twist,
Leaves quiver as if they missed.
The ground shakes with merry cheer,
Inviting all to gather near.

Grinning Boughs in the Breeze

Branches grinning, swaying free,
Joining in a jolly spree.
The sunbeams dance on bark so tall,
As shadows stretch and gently crawl.

With every gust, a burst of sound,
Nature's joy is all around.
Ricocheting through each bright space,
Leaves erupt with laughing grace.

Joyful Echoes of Nature's Heart

Echoes ringing, pure delight,
Rippling echoes, soft and bright.
A chirping bird just cracks a joke,
While rabbits giggle, hearts awoke.

Laughter bubbles, skipping by,
As the clouds float in the sky.
Nature's rhythm, warm and sweet,
Makes the world feel light on feet.

The Gleeful Aroma of Nature

In a garden where daisies dance,
The flowers giggle, a merry prance.
Breezes tickle the leaves above,
Nature is laughing, it's full of love.

Bees buzz in a cheerful tune,
Chasing shadows beneath the moon.
Every petal shares a grin,
A joyful world where fun begins.

Rabbits bounce with fluffy glee,
Squirrels chatter, oh so free.
Colors swirl in a bright parade,
Life's a joke that nature made.

With every rustle, a laugh appears,
Echoes of joy that fill our ears.
In this realm of silliness, we roam,
Together we find our happy home.

Chirps and Chuckles Among the Brambles

In the thicket, laughter brews,
With chirps and chuckles, nature hues.
The brambles shake with every quip,
As critters share a funny script.

A hedgehog rolls, a clumsy friend,
Crickets laugh as they pretend.
Every rustling leaf is wise,
Whispering jokes beneath the skies.

Frogs leap high with a croaky cheer,
While dragonflies buzz, oh so near.
Tales of folly twist and twine,
In every branch, punchlines align.

Beneath the stars, we share a jest,
With every chuckle, hearts feel blessed.
Amid the thorns, there's mirth to find,
Joy's woven deep in the wild's kind.

Giggly Shadows and Silhouettes

In twilight's glow, shadows play,
They dance and giggle, come what may.
With every flicker from the breeze,
Laughter whispers through the trees.

A moonbeam runs, a playful chase,
Tickling stars in the night's embrace.
Each silhouette bursts with delight,
Crafting mischief in the night.

Crickets sing a silly song,
Joining in where shadows throng.
In the laughter of the dark,
We find a joy, a little spark.

Chasing giggles, the night grows old,
With every story, tales retold.
In the calm, our hearts unite,
In shadows filled with pure delight.

The Amusing Aura of Deciduous Trees

From ancient roots, their jokes unwind,
Thick trunks twist with humor defined.
Leaves shimmer, snagging sunlit beams,
Whispering laughter, weaving dreams.

Branches stretch, they point and tease,
Collaborating with the gales and breeze.
In every rustle, their stories unfold,
Of silly squirrels and tales of old.

As autumn slaps on a colorful coat,
The trees chuckle as the leaves float.
They toss their jokes on the chilly air,
Enticing laughter everywhere.

In their embrace, we tilt and sway,
Nature's humor on display.
In the canopy, we find joy's key,
In the sunny warmth of the leafy spree.

The Happy Noise of Nature's Stage

In the forest, critters play,
With frogs that leap and squirrels sway.
A babbling brook sings a tune,
While bees dance 'round a flower's bloom.

The wind does tickle the leaves' edge,
As woodland friends form a fun pledge.
To share their jokes and silly pranks,
Creating giggles from hidden banks.

A chipmunk tells a joke so sly,
While owls hoot their laughter high.
Even the rocks start to chuckle,
As nature's stage leads to a tussle.

From morning light to evening's fall,
The laughter echoes, embracing all.
In every nook, a jest unfolds,
A joyful world of tales retold.

Mirthful Moments at Dusk

As day departs, the crickets cheer,
With chirps and chirrups loud and clear.
Fireflies wink with playful glee,
While shadows dance, wild and free.

A raccoon shares a joke with the thrush,
Amidst the rush of twilight's hush.
Every leaf begins to sway,
To the rhythm of dusk's ballet.

Squirrels slip on mossy trails,
Chasing after tales of fails.
Underneath a twinkling sky,
Fluffy clouds drift as they sigh.

With laughter ringing in the air,
Each moment sparkles, free from care.
The night wraps snug all playful hearts,
As mirth and magic never parts.

Prismatic Giggles Under the Sun

In the meadow, colors gleam,
As butterflies chase a sunbeam.
The daisies nod, their heads so bright,
Creating laughter, pure delight.

A rabbit hops in a silly race,
While bees paint smiles on every face.
With joyful jumps and vibrant plays,
They add to sunshine's merry rays.

A group of ants form a parade,
On tiny shoulders, dreams are made.
With giggles soft and cheerful hums,
Nature's laughter sweetly comes.

In playful hues, the world does spin,
With every chuckle, joy moves in.
Each moment holds a twinkling grin,
As life unveils where fun begins.

The Woodland's Whispered Joys

Beneath the boughs where shadows play,
The creatures laugh throughout the day.
A whispered joke, a fluttering wing,
Each giggle blooms, a joyful spring.

With acorns dropped, a playful mess,
The forest teems with happiness.
The wind conveys a gentle tease,
Tickling everyone with a breeze.

The mushrooms chuckle, round and proud,
As laughter swells beneath the cloud.
The playful sounds of chirps arise,
Beneath the gaze of sunset skies.

In every nook, great tales emerge,
With woodland joys that softly surge.
From twinkling stars to dawn's first light,
The woodland whispers, pure delight.

Foliage Filled with Giggles

In a grove where shadows dance,
Leaves sway with a cheeky prance.
Breezes whisper silly jokes,
As the tree trunk gently pokes.

Branches twist in playful glee,
While acorns roll off laughing free.
Mushrooms chuckle, grass joins in,
In this fun where all can grin.

Squirrels leap from limb to limb,
With giggles trailing on a whim.
The sunlight beams with a grin wide,
In this place where joy can't hide.

When the moon rises, shadows twirl,
It's a giggly, leafy whirl.
Foliage echoes, the night is bright,
With laughter sparkling like starlight.

Smiles in the Starlit Forest

Underneath the shimmering sky,
Trees stretch up and seem to sigh.
Whispers of laughter float through air,
Crickets chirp without a care.

Moonbeams bounce on branches high,
Inviting all to join and try.
Owl hoots a riddle in the dark,
While fireflies giggle, leaving a spark.

Winds fling giggles around the glade,
As shadows dance, unafraid.
Every twig and twiglet hums,
In laughter, the forest becomes.

As night deepens, fun's not done,
In this haven, joy will run.
Nature's humor fills the place,
With every beat, a smiling face.

Ticklish Twigs at Dusk

At dusk, the twigs start to sway,
They giggle softly, come what may.
With every tickle of the breeze,
They giggle loud among the trees.

The leaves rustle in wild delight,
As squirrels play a game at night.
Branches jostle, tickled by stars,
Creating fun beneath Mars.

Beneath the canopy, a whimsy show,
With every shake, more laughter flows.
Rabbits burst forth, joining the cheer,
In a world where all can hear.

The dusk is a time for playful tease,
Where nature's charm puts hearts at ease.
With every chuckle and every sway,
The twigs keep giggling till break of day.

The Secret Laughter of Branches

High above in tangled nests,
Branches share their secret quests.
In hush of night, they softly snicker,
With echoes that can make hearts quicker.

A woodpecker's tap sounds like applause,
As leaves shake with little cause.
In the twilight, they play a trick,
With whispers that dance, quick and slick.

These sturdy limbs, they sway and bend,
In the night, they blend and mend.
Crickets join the merry play,
While branches giggle 'til the day.

Their laughter lingers, soft and light,
A secret joy in the cool, dark night.
Nature's humor, a woven thread,
In every leaf, the laughter spreads.

Joyful Grooves of the Forest

In the woods where shadows play,
Trees dance with delight each day.
Squirrels giggle, leaping high,
While leaves whisper their secret sighs.

Moss carpets the ground with cheer,
Echoing laughter that we hear.
Rabbits trot in a silly way,
Joining in the fun of the day.

Where Gnarled Roots Laugh

Roots like fingers stretched below,
Winking at all who wander slow.
They curl and twist with a clever grin,
Cracking jokes as the day begins.

Mushrooms chuckle in their bright hats,
Dancing around the curious rats.
Every nook has a tale to tell,
In this place where giggles swell.

Chortling in the Woodland Depths

Deeper down where the sun is shy,
Creatures gather, oh my, oh my!
A raccoon jests with a sly little face,
While owls hoot in a comic embrace.

Beneath the ferns, with a peek and a wink,
The chortles rise; what do you think?
Every rustle is filled with glee,
In this woodland of pure jubilee.

The Humor Woven in Twigs

Twigs twist together in a merry knot,
Whispering tales of the funny and hot.
A hedgehog rolls, all prickles and fun,
Chasing the shadows that spring in the sun.

Branches sway with a boisterous creak,
Tickling the skies with a jovial peek.
Sticks tap dance on a soft moss bed,
In this world where laughter is fed.

Detailed Ditties of the Rolling Pines

Among the trees, a tale is spun,
A swaying dance, oh what fun!
The branches giggle in the breeze,
Tickling bark, oh, if you please.

A squirrel jokes, with acorn in tow,
Telling birds, just watch me go!
The forest chuckles, roots entwined,
With laughter shared, they feel aligned.

Oh, piney whispers, light and free,
Echoing through the canopy.
Each rustle tells of silly plight,
As shadows bounce in pure delight.

Underneath the giggling shade,
Nature's humor serenely played.
In every nook, a prankster's glee,
Rolling pines, forever merry.

Witty Whispers in the Wilderness

In shadows deep, where secrets hide,
A chattering breeze, a joyous ride.
The leaves confide in playful songs,
With every twist, where laughter throngs.

The owls exchange their cheeky notes,
While rabbits wear their silly coats.
A fox prances, a jester bold,
Telling tales, both bright and old.

Squirrels chatter, a comic troupe,
Spinning gags in a leafy loop.
The moon grins down with playful light,
Joining in this whimsical night.

Through trees enchanted, laughter flows,
As nature cracks its witty prose.
Each shout and giggle fills the air,
In wilderness, it's fun to share.

Frothy Frolics of the Old Beech

Beneath the boughs of the wise old beech,
Silly whispers are within reach.
The mossy patches burst with cheer,
While critters laugh, they gather near.

A raccoon juggles fallen fruits,
As elder trees sport leafy suits.
The sunbeams chuckle, dance on leaves,
While nature's heart, a joke weaves.

With every rustle, giggles swell,
In every nook, a secret spell.
The roots, they twist in playful lays,
Creating fun in myriad ways.

As twilight falls, the stories flow,
With frothy tales, the beech will glow.
In its embrace, the laughter thrives,
All frolicking like joyful lives.

Comedic Companionship in the Cedars

In cedar realms, where jesters meet,
The thickets hum with laughter sweet.
A gaggle of geese, on a winged spree,
Flap and honk, oh what a glee!

The cedars chuckle, tall and proud,
While the winds shout jokes aloud.
A playful breeze, a ticklish game,
Brings forth laughter, no two the same.

Beneath their shade, friends will find,
Comedic moments, nature's kind.
With bark that beams, and leaves that sway,
In companion humor, we find our way.

So join the fun, don't be shy,
In playful company, we can fly.
The cedars grin, their stories spun,
In this green stage, the joy's not done!

Jolly Shadows in the Green

In the trees where giggles grow,
A squirrel dances on a toe.
Laughter echoes from the leaves,
As sunlight winks and softly weaves.

Beneath the branches, shadows play,
Chasing each other day by day.
A rabbit jokes with a wise old crow,
While butterflies spin in a funny show.

Mossy stones wear silly hats,
Chattering quietly like old chitchats.
Every corner holds a smile,
Nature's fun is worth the while.

So come and join this playful spree,
Where even the flowers giggle with glee.
In jolly shadows, the green does gleam,
A world so bright, it's like a dream.

Fun and Frolic in the Forest

Whiskers twitch in merry delight,
Tree trunks tickle with all their might.
The woodland dances, swaying around,
As laughter bubbles up from the ground.

Frogs wear ties in the muddy bog,
And dance with snails in a twinkling fog.
A fox pulls pranks on the moonlit trail,
While fireflies flicker like a fairy tale.

Leaves burst into a bubbling cheer,
Each whisper stirs up another sneer.
The owls hoot jokes that make one urk,
In the forest, mirth is grand work.

From peaks to valleys, joy does stretch,
In every nook, a burst or sketch.
So roam the woods, let giggles soar,
For fun and frolic forevermore.

Radiant Roars of the Wild

Beneath the shade of chortling trees,
Lions chuckle in the morning breeze.
Their roars are faultless, funny and bright,
As they prance in the warm sunlight.

Zebras wear stripes like a silly suit,
While monkeys swing in a playful loot.
The rhinos stomp in a giggling race,
Nature revels in this wild embrace.

Giraffes share secrets from lofty heights,
Exchanging winks on starry nights.
Even the ants in a line parade,
Join the chorus of laughter they've made.

So hear the wild laugh, it's no façade,
In radiant roars, joy is unflawed.
March with the creatures, unleash a cheer,
In the heart of nature, nothing to fear.

The Playful Pathways of Nature

Paths twist and turn, a whimsical maze,
Where beetles brag in a charming craze.
The daisies giggle, heads held high,
While butterflies flutter, oh my, oh my!

Winding trails of light and shade,
Hold stories and pranks that never fade.
A hedgehog dons a tiny cap,
And rolls away with a little clap.

The brook chuckles as it flows,
Telling tales that everyone knows.
With each splash, pure joy arrives,
In this playground where laughter thrives.

So skip along, don't miss a step,
On pathways where nature's humor leapt.
With every glance, cheerful sights await,
In playful worlds where joy does create.

Heartfelt Chuckles Hidden in the Underbrush

In the shade where shadows dance,
Little critters twist and prance.
A squirrel snickers, a rabbit grins,
Laughter bubbles where fun begins.

Leaves whisper secrets, giggles abound,
Nature's humor can easily be found.
A toad croaks jokes in rhythmic croon,
While fireflies flicker a playful tune.

Playful Spirits of the Grove

A breeze teases branches with a tickle,
While hidden sprites share a little trickle.
The owls hoot jokes that make them grin,
As the sun dips down, the fun begins.

With mushrooms smiling on soft, green beds,
The laughter echoes above their heads.
Dancing shadows play hide and seek,
In this grove, it's the laughter that speaks.

The Silly Symphony of Saplings

Tiny trees sway in perfect time,
Their roots tap dance in rhythm sublime.
A gentle rustle, a joyous cheer,
The saplings giggle, drawing near.

With twigs as batons, they conduct the air,
Their leafy laughter is free and rare.
And as each breeze plays a new refrain,
Their silly symphony echoes again.

Glee Among the Gnarled Ones

In twisted wood where wise trees stand,
Joyful whispers from branches grand.
With knots and grooves, they tell a tale,
Of playful winds that send them sailing.

The old bark bends with a knowing grin,
A cackle of crows joins in the din.
As shadows stretch and the day turns night,
The gnarled ones laugh, a humorous sight.

Promenade of Peculiar Sounds

In the woods where whispers play,
Each tree has jokes for the day.
The branches sway with silly glee,
As squirrels giggle, wild and free.

A rustling leaf laughs in the breeze,
Tickling the bushes, oh what a tease!
Mushrooms dance in a merry row,
While shadows giggle, putting on a show.

The brook will bubble with mirthful cheer,
Echoing laughter, loud and clear.
With every step, the ground will sing,
Of vibrant joy, and the fun it brings.

So come along and join the fun,
Where silly sounds are never done.
Nature's humor, a wondrous art,
Life's a joke, a joyful part.

The Light-hearted Language of Leaves

Leaves gossip with a tickling sound,
Brushing softly against the ground.
They snap their fingers, oh so bright,
In conversations of pure delight.

A breeze arrives, full of cheer,
With secrets whispered to the ear.
The foliage chuckles, swaying wide,
In this warm, embracing glide.

Sunlight drips like honey sweet,
Each ray, a giggle, a joyful treat.
The playfulness in the air so true,
Makes hearts lift with every hue.

Every rustle tells a tale,
Of silly winds that never fail.
Join the laughter, don't be shy,
The language of leaves will never die.

Cheerful Charms of the Wildwood

In the heart of the wildwood's play,
Charming creatures dance and sway.
With blinks and winks, they spread their cheer,
A joyful crowd, bring on the year!

The rabbits giggle, hopping near,
While owls hoot, "Come join us here!"
Each corner brims with happy sights,
As nature throws its wild delights.

Beneath the boughs, tales unfold,
Of playful spirits, brave and bold.
Every flower wears a grin,
As bees buzz loudly, drawing in.

So skip along this merry lane,
Where laughter drowns in playful rain.
Embrace the whimsy, let it bloom,
In wildwood's laughter, find your room.

Tumbling Laughter in Springtime

Fresh blooms burst with giggles bright,
Painting the world in pure delight.
The sun beams down with a sparkling wink,
While rivers dance and gently shrink.

Breezes tickle flowers in a row,
As blossoms chat in the twilight glow.
Each petal whispers jokes on air,
Inviting all to stop and stare.

Little critters join the spree,
Chasing shadows, wild and free.
With every hop and cheerful squeak,
The spirit of spring, so bold, unique.

As laughter tumbles down the hills,
A symphony of joyous thrills.
In this season, full of cheer,
The world is bright, with laughter near.

Whispers of the Wooden Grin

In the glade where the branches sway,
A treelet giggles, in its own way.
With each rustle, a chuckle climbs,
Echoing softly, in quirky rhymes.

The squirrels dance, with nimble feet,
While the bark rolls over, feeling sweet.
A ticklish breeze, through the leaves it twirls,
Spreading laughter, as nature unfurls.

Beneath the shade, shadows perform,
A puppet show, in perfect form.
The roots shake hands with the little ones,
Embracing laughter, with no need for puns.

In this haven where mirth is found,
The trees join in, with a joyful sound.
All flora together, in a merry rot,
Life is a jest, in this leafy plot.

Laughter Rooted in Shadows

Amidst the trees, shadows play hide,
Where whispers of joy and chuckles reside.
The ivy's grin and the moss's tease,
Craft a chorus, with such perfect ease.

A branch bows down, as if to jest,
Tickling the ground, in genuine quest.
Forest folk giggle, a delightful sound,
Where silly antics of life abound.

Chipmunks chortle, their cheeks all full,
While the oak's belly shakes, what a pull!
With knotted knots and a twisty frame,
Each barked laugh calls out a name.

Beneath the boughs where stories intertwine,
The laughter grows, like roots entwined.
Oh, how the woods burst into glee,
For ancient jokes that set them free.

Echoes of a Playful Timber

A woodsy giggle drifts through the air,
Where trunks grouch and bark shares a dare.
The leaves snicker, they swirl and twine,
In sap-sweet tales, all woven fine.

A dappled sunbeams breaks into fits,
As treefolk gather, and humor hits.
The saplings laugh, all young and spry,
They jump and jive, reaching for the sky.

Knotted jokes in branches lie,
Tickling the clouds that float on by.
Nature's punchlines tumble and roll,
Each chuckle a spark, igniting the whole.

With roots that tickle and bark that grins,
The forest giggles, where joy begins.
Among the trees where laughter flows,
Every whisper dances, and merriment grows.

Smiles Amongst the Canopy

In a leafy realm where stories weave,
The trees chuckle, it's hard to believe.
With smiles that bloom, they lightly sway,
Sharing wisdom in the silliest way.

The limbs toss banter, a playful jest,
Swinging with glee, feeling quite blessed.
While playful shadows skip to the beat,
The forest floor hums, a rhythmic treat.

In laughter's embrace, twigs shake with glee,
As birds drop hints of pure jubilee.
Nimbly they flit, through branches and boughs,
Each chirp and chuckle, a brightening wow.

With each gust of wind, soft giggles roam,
Creating a scene that feels like home.
In this harmony, where smiles align,
The joyous canopy—nature's design.

Frolicsome Signs in the Silhouettes

In shadows of the dancing trees,
A giggle whispers on the breeze.
Branches sway with mirthful glee,
Nature's jesters, wild and free.

Leaves rustle in joyful play,
Life's a game in bright array.
Silly shapes in twilight's hue,
Serenading the stars anew.

Roots twist in a playful jig,
The ground beneath a swaying twig.
Every crack, a secret laugh,
Nature's joy, a vibrant path.

Smiling boughs in every fold,
A tale of joy gently told.
With every creak, a chuckle rings,
Life's a dance with wondrous things.

Laughter Lurking in the Green

Beneath the leafy canopy,
Giggles hide in harmony.
Dancing blades in playful waltz,
Nature's cheer, no faults at all.

Frogs sing songs of merry cheer,
While crickets chirp for all to hear.
A rustle here, a chuckle there,
Joy abounds, light as air.

The sunbeams peek, they join the jest,
Creating warmth, a golden fest.
In every breeze, a witty spark,
Nature's mirth, lighting the park.

Old trees crack jokes, with a grin,
Whispering laughter deep within.
A tapestry of joy unfurls,
In the green, where laughter swirls.

The Amused Whisperings of Saplings

Young branches wag, so full of glee,
Softly giggling, 'Look at me!'
With every sway, they spin and twirl,
Joyful whispers in a whirl.

Buds hold secrets, waiting to bloom,
Tickling the air with fragrant perfume.
In a world so bright and gay,
Saplings dance the day away.

Sunlight dapples, highlights their cheer,
Casting shadows, fun is near.
With each breeze, they nod and wink,
Little pranksters, don't you think?

Drawing smiles from passerby,
Swaying leaves catch the eye.
Nature's jesters, young and spry,
In their laughter, spirits fly.

Chuckles Carved in Knots

Twisted trunks with stories to tell,
In every knot, there's laughter to dwell.
Old wood chuckles at time's embrace,
Lines of joy, time can't erase.

A gnarled branch lifts in delight,
Sharing giggles with the night.
Under moon's soft, glowing glance,
Ancient trees sway in a dance.

The wise old oak cracks a grin,
Mirthful echoes in the wind.
Each twist a tale of silly lore,
A history rich, forevermore.

With every bark, a chuckle's found,
A joyful symphony surrounds.
In nature's hub, where laughter stays,
Knots of joy brighten our days.

Giggles from the Timbered Heights

In the woods so deep and bright,
A tree laughed with sheer delight,
Its branches danced in breezy glee,
Tickling all who passed by free.

Squirrels paused to hear the sound,
While birds burst forth, their voices drowned,
Each rustle brought a chuckle new,
As nature played its merry tune.

The leaves would shimmy, twist and twirl,
While critters joined in nature's whirl,
A symphony of silly fun,
In the shade of the brightening sun.

So if you wander through the glade,
Listen close, don't be afraid,
For you might hear a jolly tree,
Giggling softly, wild and free.

The Folly of the Laughing Branches

High above where shadows creep,
Branches crackle, secrets leap,
"Who's that dancing?" they might shout,
Only squirrels with tails about.

A raccoon peeks with beady eyes,
Wondering if the dance implies,
A feast of nuts, a wild parade,
In this leafy, fun charade.

Each gust of wind, a playful cheer,
With every twist, we shed a tear,
For laughter bubbles, fills the air,
Where silly pranks are everywhere.

In the timber, joy abounds,
With cracking limbs and playful sounds,
Nature's jesters, wild and free,
Whisper jokes from leaf to tree.

Whimsy Wrapped in Bark

Snuggled in the old oak's embrace,
Laughter bubbles, leaves interlace,
Beneath the boughs, the laughter flows,
In whispers, songs of joy it sows.

The shadows chuckle as they play,
And sunbeams giggle on their way,
Dancing light in patches bright,
Twirling leaves take joyful flight.

Acorns haul their joyful tune,
While chipmunks hum beneath the moon,
In this forest, humor reigns,
As every creature shares its gains.

So wander near the trees today,
Join the fun that comes your way,
For in the woods, a smile will spark,
A whimsy wrapped in every bark.

The Jester of the Tree Line

Along the edge where trees convene,
A jester laughs, both bright and keen,
With every branch that creaks and shakes,
Delightful pranks the forest makes.

Laughter echoes on the breeze,
With every sway among the leaves,
The jester waves, a leafy crowd,
As nature sings, and joy is loud.

From twig to twig, a dance unfolds,
In tales of mischief yet untold,
Each wind-blown joke a fleeting jest,
In this world, it's smiles that fest.

So heed the jester, join the jest,
Embrace the joy, feel truly blessed,
For in the woods, you'll find the cheer,
In every laugh that draws you near.

Laughter Wrapped in Roots

In a glade where shadows play,
The roots begin to sway,
They giggle in the morning light,
Tickling toes, a joyful sight.

Bubbles of laughter rise and fall,
Echoes dance and gently call,
Nature's jesters, wild and free,
Sharing jokes with every tree.

Giggling Underneath the Boughs

Underneath the leafy shade,
Whispers float, a fun parade,
Branches bow with silly grace,
Smiles adorn each mushy face.

Breezes carry chuckles near,
As squirrels scamper with good cheer,
The laughter sprawls from limb to limb,
In this forest, life's a whim.

The Sprightly Trunks

Sprightly trunks, so stout and grand,
Joke with leaves, a lively band,
They wobble as the wind does tease,
Shaking off the morning freeze.

A punchline here, a quip with style,
Bark and laughter mix a while,
Every crack a joyful sound,
Nature's humor all around.

Mirthful Murmurs of Nature

Mirthful murmurs swirl the air,
Frolicsome whispers everywhere,
Each creature chips in with delight,
Making mischief day and night.

A chorus of glee among the green,
Chortles echo in between,
Beneath the canopy so wide,
Laughter lives, a gentle guide.

Echoes of Joy in Timber

In the woodland, laughter roams,
Joyful squeaks and playful gnomes.
Branches sway with cheerful grace,
Nature's giggles fill the space.

Roots entwined in silly dance,
Whispered jokes cause hearts to prance.
Sunlight winks through leafy cheers,
Echoes of delight through years.

Bark that wears a toothy grin,
Rustles tales of playful sin.
Squirrels chuckle, birds retort,
Life's a joyful, wild sport.

In this grove of mirthful cheer,
Every creature finds a peer.
Wonders rise with every breeze,
In this place of giggling trees.

The Grinning Grove

In the shade of leafy friends,
Laughter's melody transcends.
Tree trunks sway in jovial fun,
Underneath the golden sun.

Boughs that creak with happy pranks,
Whisper secrets in their ranks.
Mice exchange their cheeky quips,
As sunlight dances on their tips.

Each fruit hangs with teasing flair,
Inviting joy to fill the air.
Nature beams with vibrant glee,
In this grove, we all feel free.

A tickle from the rustling leaves,
Woven tales make heartstrings weave.
In laughter's embrace, we partake,
This grove's delight we never shake.

Chuckles Among the Leaves

Among the branches, jokes take flight,
While owls hoot with pure delight.
Leaves converse with giggles bright,
In a magical, leafy night.

Acorns roll down with a cheer,
Whispers of laughter seem to steer.
A rabbit grins, a fox grins wide,
Sharing secrets, side by side.

The breeze joins in, a gentle tease,
As nature plots its clever schemes.
Frogs croak punchlines near the brook,
In this forest, joy's the hook.

Chuckles bursting from each nook,
Every corner's bound to look.
In the heart of Nature's throw,
Laughter rings through all we know.

Trees That Tell Jokes

Sturdy trunks with tales to spin,
Beneath the bark, the fun begins.
With every rustle, every laugh,
Nature crafts its merry path.

Branches stretch with a playful tease,
Whispering laughter on the breeze.
The wind composes a joyful tune,
Under the watchful eye of the moon.

Tall tales shared from boughs so high,
While the night critters chip and sigh.
With every grin, the stars align,
In this wood, all worlds entwine.

Even roots giggle underground,
Where the deepest chuckles abound.
In this forest full of glee,
Every heartbeat feels so free.

The Jester's Heart Within the Oaks

In the trees where the wild winds play,
Laughter dances in a bright array.
The branches sway with a joy so grand,
Echoing giggles across the land.

Squirrels prance with a comic flair,
Chasing shadows without a care.
With every twist and playful bound,
A jester's heart is surely found.

Beneath the canopy, secrets unfold,
Of silly tales and tricks retold.
Whispers float on a summer breeze,
Making mirth with the rustling leaves.

So join the fun in the leafy glades,
Where silliness and joy never fades.
With every bark, a laugh ignites,
In the heart of oak, pure delight takes flight.

Revelry in the Rooted Realm

In a patch where the old roots twist,
Laughter rises; you can't resist.
Frogs wear hats and dance in line,
As fireflies twinkle, all divine.

Each grounded jest, a whimsy grand,
Comes forth from deep within the sand.
With giggles echoing through the night,
The rooted realm springs pure delight.

Mice in shoes tap a merry beat,
While crickets play their playful treat.
Amidst the bushes, stories bloom,
Creating joy that chases gloom.

So let the revels rise and soar,
In nature's kingdom, forevermore.
With every chuckle, we find our place,
In the rooted realm of endless grace.

The Dappled Laughs of Daylight

Sunlight spills through the leafy green,
Casting shadows that dance and preen.
Laughter ripples along the stream,
As nature joins in the cheerful dream.

Chirping birds in their own cabaret,
Sing silly songs to brighten the day.
Bumblebees tickle the blooming flowers,
Bringing joy in spring's happy hours.

With every bounce of the dappled light,
A symphony of giggles ignites.
The sun winks down with a cheeky jest,
Nature chuckles at its very best.

So dance with shadows, laugh on the way,
In this playful world where frolics play.
Let joy spread wide from bright to stark,
In the dappled laughs, the world's silly spark.

Nature's Whimsical Revelations

In the woods where the wild things sing,
Whispers of joy make the heart take wing.
Rabbits twirl with playful grace,
Frolicking in this enchanted space.

The clouds wear smiles as they drift by,
Tickling the trees and the open sky.
With every breeze comes a gentle tease,
Nature's secrets put us at ease.

A brook giggles with a splashing sound,
As it tumbles and leaps on the ground.
The sun joins in, with a silly grin,
While flowers sway with a joyful spin.

In this realm of playful mirth,
Every step feels like a new rebirth.
So take a moment, let laughter reign,
In nature's whimsical, joyous domain.

Playful Echoes of the Evergreens

In the woods where whispers tease,
Laughter dances with the breeze.
Sprightly shadows leap and bound,
Joyful giggles all around.

Spruce trees sway in merry glee,
Wobbling branches, wild and free.
A chorus of chuckles in the air,
Nature's jesters unaware.

Sunlight twinkles on the floor,
As pine cones roll out, hoping for more.
Squirrels scamper with a jest,
Nature's fun invites a quest.

Beneath the boughs, a secret lay,
A laughing brook with games to play.
Each ripple a story, bright and clear,
Echoing laughter, drawing near.

The Snickering Stillness of Nature

Silent creeks hold secrets tight,
Rippling with mischief, pure delight.
Moonlit paths that twist and twirl,
Nature's jest starts to unfurl.

Crickets chirp their little puns,
Underneath the glowing suns.
Leaves are chuckling, shifting light,
In the heart of the quiet night.

Every rustle tells a joke,
Mossy stones begin to poke.
The owls hoot with knowing smiles,
While shadows dance in gleeful piles.

In stillness, nature plays her role,
Riddles whispered, pure and whole.
Beneath the calm, the laughter grows,
In hidden nooks where joy just flows.

Grasslands with a Grin

Waves of green that laugh and sway,
Fields of humor, bright as day.
With dandelions' cheeky flair,
Tickling toes with gentle air.

Whimsical winds brush past the reeds,
Carrying laughter, planting seeds.
Bumblebees buzz with cheeky cheer,
In sunny corners, fun draws near.

The daisies wink, a cloth of white,
Playful petals dancing bright.
The hills hum tunes both soft and sweet,
Where rolling laughs to rhythms meet.

Beneath a sky so full of mirth,
Each blade of grass reveals its worth.
Nature chuckles with open glee,
In grassy realms where hearts roam free.

Whimsical Wonders Beneath the Pines

Underneath the towering trees,
Whispers float on fragrant breeze.
Mushrooms giggle in a row,
As cheeky critters steal the show.

Pinecones drop with playful sound,
Rolling softly on the ground.
Each step a titter, each path a jest,
In nature's arms, we find our rest.

The shadows play in hide and seek,
A rustle here, a playful peek.
Squirrels chatter, plotting tricks,
In the woodlands, jesters mix.

Beneath the boughs, a smile blooms,
Laughter echoes, dispels the glooms.
In the pines, joy's not obscure,
Adventure waits, a heart so pure.

The Merry Canopy Above

In the trees, whispers dance,
Leaves giggle in the breeze.
Twigs play hide and seek,
Laughter rustles with ease.

Squirrels wear tiny hats,
Chasing shadows all day.
A playful game of tag,
In their own furry way.

Sunbeams dip and twirl,
Painting smiles on the ground.
Nature's jesters frolic,
In their joy, we're all bound.

With every branch and bough,
A chuckle lingers near.
The canopy above us,
Whispers fun in each ear.

Nature's Quirky Soundtrack

Crickets play the fiddle,
In the twilight's embrace.
A chorus of caws and chirps,
In this merry place.

Frogs croon a silly tune,
Hopping to the beat.
While fireflies twinkle like stars,
Dancing on their feet.

The wind hums a playful tune,
As leaves start to sway.
Nature's silly ensemble,
Makes us laugh and play.

A symphony of giggles,
Echoing through the trees.
Where every note is joyful,
Put your worries at ease.

Delightful Rhythms of the Earth

The ground gives a gentle shake,
As worms do a little jig.
Mushrooms wear caps so bright,
While ants form a big league.

Clouds puff up like cotton,
In a race against the sun.
Puffs of fluff with a chuckle,
Joined together for fun.

Raindrops tap on the roof,
Like tiny little feet.
Each splash brings a giggle,
Making the day sweet.

In every nook and cranny,
Nature shows its mirth.
A joyful, grand ballet,
This quirky little earth.

Raucous Revelry Among the Bark

Barks of laughter echo loud,
Where trees throw a grand ball.
Branches twist and twirl about,
    As critters start to crawl.

A raccoon with a top hat,
    Dances 'round a trunk.
While owls hoot the music,
    Their wit, the perfect funk.

The party swings and sways,
With shadows swirling bright.
Nature's revelers make merry,
    Under the moonlight.

From the roots to the sky,
Every creature with glee.
Celebrating together,
    In this wild jubilee.

Euphoria in the Enchanted Boughs

Upon the branches, giggles sprout,
Leaves dance lightly, twist about.
The sun peeks in with a cheeky grin,
Nature's laughter, where joy begins.

Squirrels prance with acorn hats,
Whispering jokes to playful brats.
Colorful blooms burst out with glee,
In this realm, all are carefree.

A breeze that carries a chuckling tone,
Invites the creatures, the wild, the lone.
The streams hum sweetly, tickling the toes,
Amidst the greens, the merriment flows.

With every rustle of foliage bright,
The woods erupt in sheer delight.
Leaves proclaim in joyful cheer,
In the boughs, there's nothing to fear.

The Vibrant Voice of Verdancy

Amidst the greenery, laughter swells,
The sapling whispers, and the tall tree yells.
Pinecones wobble, ready for flight,
As the forest chuckles under the light.

Daffodils wiggle, not wanting to stand,
Sunshine tickles, a warm, gentle hand.
With every breeze, stories unfold,
Of frolicsome sprites and warriors bold.

Mushrooms giggle, hiding in nooks,
Sharing their tales in cunning books.
Chirping crickets add to the song,
In this vibrant land, we all belong.

The bushes shiver, full of surprise,
As butterflies dance in whimsical ties.
Every shadow holds a tiny jest,
In the verdant world, we feel so blessed.

Trees with a Sense of Humor

Tall trunks stand, wearing sly smirks,
Branched-out jokes from nature's works.
A rustle of leaves, a tickle of air,
Each tree's secret fills the square.

Birches tease the passing streams,
As willows giggle, lost in dreams.
The oaks are wise, with winks in their bark,
Sharing punchlines in twilight's dark.

A pine can crack a rugged line,
While maples flourish, feeling divine.
In every grove, a joke is spun,
Under the moon, the laughter's begun.

Among the woods, great spirits arise,
With every chuckle, good humor lies.
Nature's jesters in green attire,
Ignite the heart with unending fire.

The Merrymaking Murk of the Forest

In the depths where shadows sway,
Frogs croon tunes, come out to play.
Echoes of joy rise on the breeze,
Laughter bubbles beneath the trees.

Muddy boots and playful splashes,
Squirrels compete in wild dashes.
Twigs snap, and the floor bursts with cheer,
Adventures await, bring friends near.

Owls wink from their leafy spots,
Sharing wisdom and funny thoughts.
Every critter, with giggles to share,
In the murk, laughter floats in the air.

As evening settles, the glowworms gleam,
Illuminating the forest's dream.
Each rustle whispers a happy tune,
In the merrymaking, we'll find our moon.

The Chortling Thicket

In shadows where the branches sway,
Laughter hides in bright array.
A squirrel jests with acorn flair,
The sunbeams giggle in the air.

Fern fronds dance with silly flair,
While snickers bounce from here to there.
A rabbit hops on tiny feet,
Tickling toes with music sweet.

Above, the jaybird's hearty call,
Echoes through the woodland hall.
With every rustle, snorts are heard,
As nature shares a joyful word.

So wander through this laughing wood,
In every nook, feel light and good.
For in these leaves where giggles thrive,
A happy spirit comes alive.

Treetop Humor and Hilarity

High above, the branches jest,
Chattering leaves, they do their best.
A playful breeze with tickled hands,
Makes tree trunks sway like merry bands.

The owl winks with a silly grin,
As squirrels scurry, chasing win.
Nutty jokes from hickory trees,
Bring chuckles soft like summer breeze.

Underfoot, the mushrooms clap,
With earthy jokes and funny nap.
While shadows dance in playful light,
Wit sprawls out to greet the night.

In every nook, the joy runs free,
Nature's comic symphony.
So hang your cares and lose your frown,
In this treetop circus town.

Joyful Rooted Revelry

Roots entwined beneath the ground,
Whisper tales that spin around.
The laughter of the earthworms grows,
As jokes upon the surface flow.

Mushrooms giggle, sprouting wise,
With (hilarious!) caps to disguise.
Daisies join in with dainty dance,
Spinning joy with every chance.

Each pebble sings a playful tune,
As flowers sway beneath the moon.
The crickets chirp their cheeky jest,
Inviting all to join the fest.

So join the roots, let laughter spread,
In this merry place, be fed.
For in the depths where humor thrives,
A joyful heart forever drives.

Lighthearted Whispers of Woodlands

Breezes tease the treetops high,
As whispers tickle, oh my, my!
The leaves conspire in silly schemes,
Chasing laughter through the dreams.

A chipmunk pranks with quick delight,
Making shadows dance at night.
The fern fronds giggle, soft and shy,
While starlit twinkles wink and sigh.

In dappled glades, the fun unfolds,
As stories shared have magic told.
The nightingale croons a comical tune,
Lifting spirits beneath the moon.

So roam these woods where laughter flows,
And joy abounds in highs and lows.
For in this land of merry cheer,
The heart finds happiness held near.

Giggling Vines in Sunlight

In the meadow where shadows play,
Giggling vines dance in bright array.
Twisting around, they tease the breeze,
Whispers of joy among the trees.

Chasing butterflies with a laugh,
Each leaf a partner in their gaff.
Sunshine beams, their laughter glows,
In nature's jest, anything goes.

Tickling petals, a riotous spree,
Jokesters twirling, wild and free.
Laughter bubbles in the warm air,
Giggling vines, a comical affair.

A Symphony of Smiles Among Leaves

Leaves drumming lightly in cheerful beats,
A symphony of smiles, the forest greets.
Branches sway, their antics arise,
Nature's jesters beneath sunny skies.

Acorns roll in a joyful race,
Frolicking creatures keeping pace.
Every rustle a chuckle, a cheer,
In this merry world, laughter's clear.

Mirth is the language of the glade,
Where pranks unfold and worries fade.
A whisper of joy in each rustling plea,
Tales of humor float harmoniously.

The Playful Spirit of the Glade

A spirit of fun wanders the glade,
In shadows and sunlight, laughter displayed.
Chirping birds join the fray,
Tickling the breeze in their playful way.

Squirrels jest with their acorn hoard,
Each nibble a jest, in jovial accord.
While flowers giggle, flapping their lips,
In the joyful dance of nature's quips.

A frolicsome breeze tickles the ground,
In the harmony of laughter, nature's found.
Where every creature bursts into song,
The spirit of play makes them all belong.

Jostling Roots with a Sense of Humor

Deep in the earth, roots twist and shout,
Jostling gently, no fear of drought.
With whimsical giggles, they wiggle and squirm,
Creating a dance that's rooted and firm.

Tapping the soil, they share a tease,
Tickling rocks with mischievous ease.
Each bump and tumble, a jest so grand,
In the rich, dark earth, they take a stand.

Together they whisper, secrets they swap,
Spreading joy with each lively plop.
In every nook, their laughter entwines,
Jostling roots with their clever designs.

www.ingramcontent.com/pod-product-compliance
Lightning Source LLC
Chambersburg PA
CBHW070751220426
43209CB00083B/730